350 Funny Hockey Slang Terms

*The Ultimate Insider Guide
to Ice Hockey Lingo
and Terminology
for Kids*

Jamie Lindberg

Introduction

Welcome to the incredible world of ice hockey!

This tiny, fun, and easy-to-read book will be your new guide to sounding like a hockey pro.

Inside, you'll find the funniest slang hockey has invented over the centuries!

From now on, you'll always know what your favorite players and commentators are talking about! From 'biscuit' to 'bottle rocket,' from 'top shelf' to 'tender,' I've gathered the coolest and most colorful phrases from the world of ice hockey.

So, find a comfortable spot and get ready to learn how to trash talk like a hockey player. Enjoy!

1. **2 and ten**

When a player breaks the rules and gets a minor penalty plus an extra ten-minute penalty for bad behavior.

2. **2-man advantage,** *or* **five on three**

When one team has two players who have to sit out because they broke the rules. Now, the other team gets to have five players skating around (not counting the goalie), while the team with penalties only has three players on the ice.

3. **5 and a game,** *or* **Major penalty**

When a player gets a penalty that makes them sit out of the game for five minutes.

4. **6x4**

A term used to describe the goal in hockey. It refers to the dimensions of the net, which are six feet wide by four feet high.

5. **Alley-oop**

When one player throws the puck very high in the air, and another player catches it and scores a goal.

6. **Anchor**

A team member whose regular errors bring the whole group down.

7. **Angling**

A way to move an opponent's player to the side in your own defense area, ensuring they stay away from the center of that zone.

8. **Apple**

When one player passes the puck to another player, who then scores a goal. The player who passes the puck gets an assist, which is a point that counts for their statistics.

9. **Assist**

Given to one or two players on the scoring team who passed, shot, or redirected the puck to the teammate who scored.

10. **Attacking zone,** *or* **Offensive zone**

The area on the ice that belongs to the other team, stretching from the blue line all the way to the boards at the end.

11. Axe

When a player is removed or taken off the team list.

12. Babysitter

When a skilled player is put on a team with two less skilled players and has to help them perform better, like acting as the team's 'babysitter'.

13. Back checking

Quickly returning to the defensive area when the other team is on the offense.

14. Backhand

A move where the player uses the backside of the stick to pass or shoot the puck.

15. Bag of Milk

An unkind term used to describe someone as overweight.

16. Banana

A strong curve at the end of a hockey stick.

17. Bandaid

A player known for frequently getting injured.

18. Bar North

When the puck strikes the top bar of the goal and flies directly upwards.

19. Bar-Down, *or* Bar-Downski, *or* Bar-in

When a player shoots the puck so hard that it hits the top of the goal and bounces down into the net, making a loud ping sound.

20. Barn

Another name for a hockey rink.

21. Barnburner

A game where lots of points are scored, and it often moves very quickly. Sometimes it's known as a Boat Race.

22. Basket

Another word for the net, where players try to score a goal.

23. **Beautician**

A player who is skilled at playing hockey and considered attractive and charming.

24. **Beauty,** *or* **Beaut**

An awesome shot. It means the player hit the puck in a really smooth and perfect way to score a goal, or it just looked amazing when they did it.

25. **Beaver Tap**

When a player taps their stick on the ice to signal the person with the puck to notice them.

26. **Bench Boss**

Another name for the coach.

27. Bench Warmer

A player who mainly stays on the side and doesn't play much in the game.

28. Bender, *or* Ankle Burner

A new player who isn't very good at skating yet, so their ankles bend when standing up because they don't have the strength or balance to keep them straight.

29. Best-on-best

This term describes a competition where the highest-skilled players are chosen to play. It's mostly used when talking about men's international sports events that include professional athletes. These events are scheduled so they don't overlap with regular league games, ensuring that the best players can take part.

30. **Birdcage**

A protective mesh attached to a helmet to guard the face.

31. **Biscuit,** *or* **Disk**

A nickname for the puck.

32. **Black ace**

A term used for a player from a lower professional league or a young player from an amateur league who is brought up to join their main NHL team during the Stanley Cup playoffs.

33. **Blocker,** *or* **Waffle pad**

The rectangular pad that a goalie wears over the hand that holds the stick.

34. **Blow A Tire**

When a player unexpectedly falls down for no clear reason.

35. **Blue line**

It's one of the two lines on the ice that divide the playing area into attacking, defending, and neutral zones.

36. **Blueliner**

A player who plays in the defensive position in a hockey game.

37. **Boarding**

When a player hits another player who cannot defend themselves, causing them to crash into the side of the rink. This move is not allowed and will result in a penalty.

38. Boards

The walls that go around the area where the game is played. Usually, the bottom part of the wall is made of wood and goes up to about your waist. The top part is made of glass or a clear plastic called plexiglass, so you can see through it.

39. Body check

When a player uses their hip or body to bump into an opponent. The goal is to either pin the opponent against the sideboards, make them fall to the ice, or just make it harder for them to handle the puck.

In men's ice hockey, body checking is usually allowed unless it's too forceful, not needed, or if it targets a player who doesn't have the puck. However, in women's ice hockey, this move is not allowed.

40. **Bottle Rocket**

When a player shoots the puck so hard and perfectly that it flies into the goal and hits the water bottle that the goalies usually keep on top of the net.

41. **Box,** *or* **Penalty box**

The place where a player must go to spend the time given for a penalty.

42. **Brawl**

A conflict where many people are fighting at the same time.

43. **Breadbasket**

The area on a goalie where their chest is. It's typically not the best spot to aim for when trying to score a goal.

44. **Breakaway**

When a player controls the puck, and only the goalie is left to beat, with no other defenders in the way.

45. **Breezers**

A name that some people use for the special pants that hockey players wear.

46. **Brick Wall**

A goalie who performs extremely well, making it seem like no one can get a goal past him.

47. **Bucket,** *or* **Brain Bucket**

What players call their helmets.

48. **Butt-ending**

When a player pokes an opponent with the end of their hockey stick. This is not allowed and leads to severe penalties, including a major penalty and being removed from the game.

49. **Butterfly**

A way a goalie plays where they kneel down to block the bottom part of the goal with their leg guards.

50. **Buzzer Beater**

A goal made right as the game's timer is about to end

51. **Cage**

A type of face protection players wear on their helmets. It's made of wire and covers the whole face so that the puck, sticks, or anything else can't hit them in the face.

52. **Can Opener**

A move where a player slides their stick between another player's legs and twists it, causing them to trip.

53. **Captain**

Usually a player with a lot of experience or who is a leader on the team. They have the special role of talking to the referees and officials about the game rules. Other players usually can't do this. In professional hockey leagues like the NHL, each team can have one captain, shown by a "C" on their shirt, and also two or three assistant captains, shown by an "A."

54. **Carom or Carom Pass**

When a player purposely shoots the puck against the boards so that it bounces to a teammate.

55. **Catcher,** *or* **Trapper,** *or* **Catching glove**

A special glove with a web design that the goalie uses. It's worn on the hand that doesn't hold the stick.

56. **Celly**

A fun term used for the little celebration players do when they score a goal.

57. **Center**

The player who mainly plays in the middle area of the ice rink.

58. **Change on the fly**

Switching out a player for someone on the bench while the game is still going, not waiting for a break before the game restarts.

59. **Charging**

When a player runs more than three steps or jumps before hitting another player with their body. This is not allowed and results in a penalty.

60. **Cheap shot**

A sneaky, unfair, and not allowed move that hurts another player, mostly done to cause harm.

61. **Check to the head**

When a player hits another player's head, which is illegal. In the NHL, if the hit comes from the side or without the other player seeing it coming, it can lead to big penalties. In other hockey leagues, any hit to the head could result in smaller or bigger penalties, and the player might have to leave the game.

62. **Checking from behind**

When a player hits another player from the back, not giving them a chance to see it coming. This move is against the rules and results in a penalty.

63. **Cherry Picker**

A player who hangs out near the middle of the ice rink, behind the other team's defense, hoping to get a clear, easy chance to score without anyone challenging them.

64. **Cherry-picker**

Someone who waits at a certain spot on the ice, hoping to get the puck and score easily without helping the rest of the team play defense or work hard.

65. **Chiclets**

A term sometimes used jokingly by hockey players to talk about teeth. Because ice hockey is a very fast and physical sport, players sometimes get hit in the mouth and can lose teeth.

66. **Chippy**

A word that people use in ice hockey when a game gets a little rough, and players from both teams start playing cheap shots that the referee is not seeing.

67. **Chirp or Beak**

Slinging clever insults and playful jabs at the other team or player, usually to throw them off their game or just for some competitive fun.

68. **Chisler**

A teammate who falsely claims to the referee that assisted on a goal to unfairly gain points.

69. **Clapper**

A powerful slapshot that makes a loud clapping sound when the player's stick hits the puck, often taken by a defenseman from far back on the ice.

70. **Clipping**

When someone hits an opponent below the knees, which is not allowed and results in a penalty.

71. **Coast-to-coast**

When a player takes the puck from around their own net, skates the entire length of the ice rink, and scores a goal without passing to a teammate.

72. Coincidental penalties

When both teams get the same number of penalties at the same time, usually during the same play or moment, but the total penalty time might not be the same for both.

73. Coughing up the puck

When someone accidentally loses control of the puck, letting the other team get it.

74. Cover 1

A strategy where one defender stays closer to the goal, ready to stop counter-attacks, while other defenders can move forward and help in attacking.

75. Crashing the net, *or* crashing the crease

A tactic where players rush toward the area in front of the goal as fast as they can. They often do this hoping to catch a rebound or get to a free puck before anyone from the other team does.

76. Crease, *or* Goal crease

A marked spot in front of the hockey net. It looks like a half-circle and is a different color. It starts at the goal line.

77. Cross Checking

A move that's not allowed, happening when a player hits another with the shaft of their stick. It has to be strong enough to result in a penalty.

78. **Cross-checking**

When someone uses their stick, holding it with both hands, to check or hit an opponent, which is not allowed and will result in a penalty.

79. **Cycling,** *or* **Cycle**

A move used in games where players pass the puck around the edges of the playing area to make a chance to score by tiring out the other team's players or getting them out of their spots.

80. **Dangle**

When a player moves the puck back and forth on their stick really fast and makes it super tricky for the other players to take it away.

81. Dasher

The boards around the rink. When a player bounces the puck off the boards to get it out of their defensive area or to pass it to another player, they're using the dasher.

82. Defenceman

The two players on the ice who stand closer to their team's goal. Their main job is to keep the area in front of their goal clear to stop the other team from scoring.

83. Defensive zone

The area controlled by the defending team. It stretches from the blue line all the way to the end boards behind the goal.

84. **Deke faint or Fake**

When a player pretends to go one way with the puck but then quickly goes the other way. This tricks the other player and makes them get out of their position. Deke is an abbreviation of the word decoy.

85. **Delayed Penalty**

When a penalty is called, and the team that broke the rules hasn't yet touched the puck to stop the game. This gives the other team a chance to replace their goalie with an extra player to help score until the team that made the mistake touches the puck. It's like getting extra penalty time.

86. **Denied**

When a goalie stops a player from scoring a goal that looked certain.

87. **Dinger**

When the player shoots the puck, it hits the metal post of the goal really hard, but doesn't go in. It's called a dinger because of the loud ding sound it makes.

88. **Dirty**

When a hockey player makes a cool and skillful move to get past another player.

89. **Dish**

A pass.

90. **Dive or Diving**

When a player pretends to be hit harder than they actually were by another player, just so they can get a penalty called.

91. **Dots**

The marked face-off spots on the ice.

92. **Draw**

A face-off, when two players from opposing hockey teams line up at a specific point on the ice and wait for the referee to drop the puck between them.

93. **Dump-and-chase**

A strategy where a team sends the puck deep into the other team's area and then quickly goes after it. This is done to get past the defense and try to score.

94. **Dust Off**

When a defenseman quickly moves the puck around.

95. Duster

Someone on the team who doesn't play often so they spend a lot of time sitting on the bench, collecting dust.

96. Dusty

A nickname for a player who sits on the bench a lot and doesn't get to skate on the ice much.

97. Egg

A game that ends 0-0.

98. Elbowing

When someone sticks out their elbow or lower arm to hit another player. This move is against the rules and results in a penalty.

99. Empty net goal, *or* Empty netter

When a goal is scored while the other team's goalie isn't on the ice.

100. Enforcer, *or* Goon, *or* Policeman

A player known for being ready to engage in fights to protect their teammates from aggressive players on the opposing team.

101. Extra attacker

When a player comes onto the ice to replace the team's goalie.

102. Face-wash

When a player rubs their glove on another player's face.

103. **Face-off**

The technique used to start the game at the opening of each period or to resume play after it has been paused. Players from the opposing teams face each other. A player from each side tries to take possession of the puck once an official releases it between their sticks over a designated spot on the rink.

104. **Face-off Spot**

The nine designated circles on the hockey rink where a faceoff can take place. There are two located in both the attacking and defending zones, two near the corners of the neutral zone, and one right at the center of the ice.

105. **Fan,** *or* **To Fan**

When a player tries to hit the puck but misses it completely.

106. Fighting, *or* Scraps, *or* Tussles, *or* Fisticuffs, *or* Scuffles, *or* Dance, *or* Donnybrook

When two or more players punch each other repeatedly. Each individual involved receives a major penalty, and this action often leads to a game misconduct penalty in numerous leagues.

107. Filthy Play

When someone makes a move or a shot that is so good, it's almost unbelievable.

108. Fishbowl

A type of protective face mask that hockey players wear. It's called a fishbowl because it's made of clear plastic and covers the whole face.

109. **Five-hole**

The space between a goalie's legs.

110. **Flamingo**

When a player tries to avoid getting hit by the puck by lifting up one leg like a flamingo.

111. **Flood**

When the ice rink is covered with a thin layer of water after the ice resurfacer has smoothed out the surface.

112. **Flow**

A term for long, vibrant hair that sticks out from under a player's helmet.

113. **For the boys (or girls),** *or* **Ferda boys**

A term used in ice hockey to describe a player who does something awesome for the sake of their teammates.

114. **Forecheck**

When a player applies pressure to the opposing team in their area of the ice to try to get the puck back and create a chance to score.

115. **Free Agent**

A hockey player who is not currently signed with any team.

116. **Freezing the puck**

When someone stops the puck and holds it so that no one else can play it.

117. **Full strength,**
or **Even strength,**
or **5-on-5**

When each team has five players and one goalie playing on the ice.

118. **Game misconduct**

A type of penalty that leads to a player's removal from the game. In terms of statistics, a player who gets a game misconduct typically receives 10 or 20 minutes worth of penalties on record.

119. **Garbage goal,**
or **Picking up the trash**

When a player scores a goal by quickly shooting the puck after it bounces off the goalie or the post. This is usually done from a very short distance, so the player does not have much time or space to aim.

120. **Getting lit up**

When a goalie is having a bad day, and the other team scores many goals on him.

121. **Gino**

A goal.

122. **Give-And-Go**

When a player passes the ball to another player and then quickly moves to get it back.

123. **Goal**

When the puck goes over the goal line in front of the net.

124. **Goal crease**

A special spot on the ice right in front of the goal net. It usually looks like a half-circle and is painted a different color to stand out. It starts from the line where goals are scored, known as the goal line.

125. **Goal judge**

An off-ice official who helps in a hockey game by showing when a goal is scored. They do this by switching on a red light that's located above the goal.

126. **Goal line**

The line that stretches from one post across to the other post. If the hockey puck goes over this line and into the net, it's counted as a goal.

127. Golden goal

A special goal in a game that, once scored during overtime, immediately ends the game with the scoring team winning.

128. Gong-show

A game that is chaotic and unpredictable. It can mean a game with a lot of physical contact, such as big hits or fights, or a game with a lot of scoring.

129. Goon, *or* Animal, *or* Cementhead, *or* Hit man, *or* Designated fighter, *or* Tough Guy

Someone who enforces the rules on the ice, but not officially. They make sure the other team doesn't play dirty or violent, and they are ready to fight back if they do. They use force without holding back to throw the other team off balance, even if it means getting penalties.

130. **Gordie Howe Hat-trick**

A goal, an assist, and a fight in one game.

131. **Greasy**

A goal that isn't pretty or a hit that's somewhat suspicious.

132. **Grenade**

A bad pass that makes it hard for the receiver to control the puck. It usually happens when the passer sends the puck too high or too fast, and it bounces or rolls on the ice before reaching the intended target.

133. **Gretzky's office**

The space right behind the goal on the ice, named after famous hockey player Wayne Gretzky because he was really good at making plays and scoring from this spot.

134. **Grinder,** *or* **Mucker**

A player known for putting in a lot of effort and being really good at defending, especially near the sides of the rink. They might not score a lot, but they're great at helping other players.

135. **Grocery stick**

A player who is so bad that he never gets to play on the ice. He just sits on the bench and separates the forwards and the defensemen, like a stick that divides the groceries on a conveyor belt at the supermarket.

136. **Gross misconduct**

A serious penalty given for extremely bad behavior that disrespects the game, happening when a player or coach acts in a way that completely mocks or ridicules the sport.

137. Half wall

Midway between the point and the corner along the board.

138. Hand pass

Moving the puck using your hand.. It's allowed when a player is within their team's defensive area but not permitted in the middle area of the rink or the offensive area. This rule applies even if the player starts the pass from a different zone.

139. Hash marks

The straight lines near the face-off circles in front of each goal. They help players line up properly for face-offs.

140. **Hat-trick,** *or* **Hatty**

When a single player scores three goals during a single game. As a way to celebrate this achievement, fans often throw their hats onto the ice.

141. **Head contact**

When someone hits a player with any part of their body or their hockey stick in the area above the shoulders, whether they meant to or not. In Canadian minor league hockey, this leads to a small penalty, or a or a double minor penalty if the hit was done on purpose.

142. **Head-butting**

When someone uses their head to hit another player on purpose or tries to score by pushing the hockey puck into the goal with their head. If a player head-butts another player, they will get a penalty. However, if they head-butt the puck into the net, it won't count as a goal.

143. **Healthy scratch**

A player who is not injured but still does not suit up to play in a game. Teams can only have 20 players (22 for games played internationally) ready to play, so those who aren't going to play are called scratches.

144. **High sticking**

1. The prohibited act of striking another player on the head or shoulders with a hockey stick. This offense results in a penalty, which is typically a minor penalty if no injury occurs, but can escalate to a more severe double minor penalty if the action causes bleeding.

2. The violation of hitting the hockey puck with one's stick when it is lifted above the shoulder level. Should a player or their teammate be the next to touch the puck after such an incident, before an opponent does, the game is immediately stopped. Moreover, any goal made because a player hits the puck with their stick over the crossbar level will not count.

145. **Hip check**

A move where you hit another player with your hip hard enough to push them against the sides of the rink or onto the ground.

146. **Hit**

Any action where a player uses their body to knock another player away from the hockey puck.

147. **Holding**

When a player grabs onto another player to stop them from moving. This is against the rules and can result in a penalty.

148. **Holding the stick**

When someone grabs an opponent's stick, which is against the rules and results in a penalty.

149. **Home-ice advantage**

The privilege to make the final line change during a game.

150. **Hooking**

When a player unfairly slows down another player by hooking the blade of their stick into the other player's body. This is against the rules and results in a penalty.

151. **Hoser**

A classic insult in hockey. It goes back to when there was no machine to clean the ice. The losers had to do the dirty work and spray water on the ice with a hose.

152. **Hot-doggers**

Players who like to show off their skills on the ice. They might try to dodge past their opponents with fancy moves or score goals with flashy shots. Doing this is called hot-dogging.

153. **House**

The space in front of the net where most scoring chances happen.

154. **Howitzer**

A powerful and quick type of hockey shot.

155. **Ice resurfacer**

A machine that fixes up the ice before and during breaks in a game to make it smooth and clean so both the puck and skates can move easily. The brand Zamboni is so famous that many people call all ice resurfacers by that name.

156. **Icing**

When a player sends the puck from behind the center red line over the opposing team's goal line, and it doesn't go into the goal or get touched by an opponent in the neutral or defensive zones.

If the puck crosses both lines like this and an opponent is the first to reach it, the game is paused by a linesman. The game starts again with a faceoff in the zone of the team that caused the stoppage.

157. **Insurance Goal**

Scoring an extra goal to make your lead bigger, giving you more space to make mistakes.

158. **Interference**

When a player who doesn't have the puck is blocked or stopped by another player in a way that's not allowed, leading to a penalty.

159. Iron cross

A defensive tactic used by a team when facing a situation where their opponents have two extra players on the ice (five-on-three). In this setup, the team arranges themselves with two defense players, one forward, and the goalie, positioning in a way that if you were to imagine lines connecting the defense players and another line connecting the forward with the goalie, these lines would create a cross shape.

This formation primarily focuses on defense, aiming to efficiently prevent the other team from scoring while the team is at a numerical disadvantage, often during a penalty situation.

160. Johnny on the spot

A term used when a player is exactly where they should be, often leading to them scoring a goal.

161. **Junk**

1. A hit to the sensitive areas of the body.

2. The corner of the goal, where the horizontal bar at the top meets the vertical post.

162. **Keep**

Another nickname for the goalie. Comes from a shorter form of the word Keeper.

163. **Kicking**

1. Moving the puck forward by hitting it with one's skates. Scoring a goal by using this technique to send the puck into the other team's goal is not allowed.

2. The action of using one's foot to kick another player. Such behavior results in an immediate match penalty.

164. **Kneeing**

When a player hits another player using their knee. This is not allowed and results in a foul.

165. **Kronwalled**

A term used to describe a big and powerful body check by a defender on an opposing player. It comes from the name of Niklas Kronwall, a former Swedish hockey player who played for the Detroit Red Wings and was known for his hard-hitting style.

166. **Laying The Lumber**

When a player hits another player with a sharp, quick motion.

167. **Left wing**

A player who stands to the left side of the center player during a game when teams have an equal number of players on the ice. This position is opposite to the right wing.

168. **Left wing lock**

A type of defense strategy similar to another strategy called the neutral zone trap. When the team loses control of the puck, the player in the left wing position quickly moves to join the defense players. Together, these three players cover the ice by dividing it into three parts, with each one taking responsibility for their own section.

Normally, a team has two defense players, so by adding the left wing, the team strengthens its defense, especially against sudden attacks by the opposing team.

169. **Lettuce**

A term used in hockey to describe a player's hair that is long and wavy, but not as long and wavy as flow.

170. **Light the lamp**

To score a goal. It comes from the red light that turns on behind the net when a goal is scored.

171. **Line**

This is a group made up of three players: a left winger, a center, and a right winger. Teams usually keep the same three players together in a line to build teamwork.

There are different types of lines for different roles, like scoring, defense, or enforcers. Some lines that have played together for a long time have become well-known, like the Russian Five and the French Connection.

172. **Line brawl**

When most or all of the players on the ice get into fights at the same time.

173. **Line change**

When one team decides to swap their offensive players or their defensive players either during the game or right after a whistle. They might do this to make sure their players don't get too tired, or to have specific players compete against certain players from the other team.

174. **Linesman,** *or* **Liney**

A game official who handles the majority of the puck drops for face-offs, and also watches for rule violations like offside and icing. They have the power to call certain penalties as well. Typically, a game will have two linesmen on the ice. In some lower-level games, there might only be two lineys and no ref, meaning they must do everything.

175. **Lip sweater,** *or* **Lip Lettuce**

A mustache.

176. **Long change**

During the second period of the game, the goalies switch sides of the rink. This makes it so the team's bench is nearer to the area where they try to score rather than where they defend.

The "long change" happens because players have to skate further to get to the bench if they're tired and need to be substituted. This can be tricky if they're stuck on the defense and can't switch out players quickly.

177. **Lumber**

A hockey stick, typically one made from wood instead of mixed materials.

178. Man advantage

When a team gets a penalty and one of its players has to go sit out in the penalty box. This means the other team gets to have one more player on the ice than the team with the penalty, until either the penalty time runs out for a big penalty or a goal is scored for a smaller penalty.

If a team gets two penalties at once, they'll be down by two players. But no matter how many penalties a team gets, they can only ever lose two players at a time for the man advantage.

179. Match penalty

A serious penalty in a game where the player is not only kicked out for five minutes, but also automatically removed from the match. Depending on the rules of the game, they might not be allowed to play in the next few games too. Match penalties are given for very bad actions like trying to hurt another player, a referee, or even a fan on purpose.

180. **Meat Wagon**

An ambulance that arrives to take a hurt hockey player to the hospital.

181. **Michigan,** *or* **High wrap,** *or* **Lacrosse move**

A cool trick in ice hockey where a player scoops up the puck on their stick and tosses it into the upper part of the goal as they skate behind it. This is usually done when the goalie is blocking the lower part of the net.

Bill Armstrong came up with this move, but Mike Legg really made it famous while he was playing for the University of Michigan. He did it so well that it's often shown in sports highlights.

182. **Minor penalty**

A type of penalty where a player has to sit out of the game for two minutes.

183. **Misconduct**

A rule in hockey where the player who breaks the rules has to leave the ice for 10 minutes. Another player can take their place during this time. Also, check out what game misconduct and gross misconduct mean for more information.

184. **Mouthy**

A protective gear worn in the mouth.

185. **Muddy Boots**

When a player seems to move slowly as if their feet are stuck in mud.

186. **Muffin**

A shot that is not very powerful or accurate but somehow manages to get past the goalie and score a goal.

187. **Munson**

The player who shows the worst behaviour during an ice hockey game.

188. **Nail**

A strong body check or a player known for being tough.

189. **Natural hat-trick**

When a player scores three goals one after another during the same period of the game.

190. **Net front presence**

A strategy where an attacker positions themselves close to the opposing team's goalie. The goal is to block the goalie's view, redirect shots coming from a distance, and grab any rebounds that the goalie may not hold onto.

191. Neutral zone

The area in the middle of the ice rink, between the blue lines.

192. Neutral zone trap

A strategic defensive technique aimed at stopping the other team from moving forward with the puck in the neutral zone, which is the space between the two blue lines, and trying to steal the puck from them.

193. Nip

Getting a goal by fitting the ball into a very small opening.

194. Odd-man rush

When one team moves into the attacking area with more players than the other team has there, like having 5 players against 4, or 3 against 2, or even 2 against 1.

195. **ODR**

An outdoor rink.

196. **Official,** *or* **Referee**

Someone who makes sure the rules are followed during a game, and they can work on the ice or from the sidelines. There are also others like linesmen and referees who help with this.

197. **Offside**

This rule is about where players are on the ice in a hockey game. When a player from the team trying to score is in the area closest to the goal before the puck gets there, and they didn't bring it in themselves, it's called offside. The play stops and only starts again once the puck or all players trying to score are out of that area.

198. **Old School Player**

A player who uses older equipment or plays in a way that isn't common anymore.

199. **Olympic Sheet of Ice**

An Olympic ice rink, which is bigger than a standard NHL ice rink. It measures 100 feet by 200 feet, while the NHL rink is 85 feet by 200 feet.

200. **One on!** (*or* **Two on,** *or* **Three on,** *or* **Man on)**

A way of warning a teammate that an opponent is approaching them from behind or the side, and they need to act fast.

201. One-man advantage,
or Five on four

When a team has one extra player because the other team has a player who can't play for some time due to a penalty.

202. One-timer

When a player shoots the puck right away after getting a pass, without playing or controlling the puck in any way.

203. Open Ice Hit

When a player is hit by an opponent in the middle of the ice rink, away from the boards.

204. Original Six

The first six teams that played in the NHL from 1942 until 1967, before more teams were added.

205. **Overcorked**

Shooting with too much force and no control.

206. **Overtime**

The additional period of play that happens after the normal game time ends if the game is tied. The game is won by the first team to score in this extra time.

207. **Own goal**

When a team accidentally scores a point in their own goal instead of the other team's. The last player from the other team who touched the puck gets credited with the goal for record-keeping.

208. **Packing A Bomb**

Throwing a ball made of used chewing tobacco in the locker room.

209. **Paddle**

The broad part at the top, just above the flat piece, on a goalie's stick in hockey.

210. **Paint**

The area around the goal where the goalie stands.

211. **Passive box**

A strategy used by a team that is missing one or more players due to a penalty. The team forms a box shape with four players in front of their goalie to protect the goal. The two players closest to the goalie are usually in charge of blocking any attempts to score from the sides or directly in front. The other two players, who are a bit further out, focus on stopping the other team's defenders from getting a clear shot and blocking passes across the ice.

All four players stay near the goal, keeping their formation the same throughout the time they are at a disadvantage, not actively chasing the opponents. This is why it's known as a "passive" box.

212. **Peanut Butter**

When a hockey puck briefly gets caught in the goal net before dropping onto the ice.

213. Penalty kill (PK)

The defensive strategies a team uses when they have fewer players on the ice because someone has been penalized. It also refers to the specific group of players who are on the ice during this time.

The main goal of these strategies is to prevent the puck from entering the team's defensive area and to play in a way that uses up the time until the penalty ends. This might mean not taking as many chances to score. Also, when a team is in this situation, the rules about icing, or sending the puck down the length of the ice from behind the center line, don't apply to them.

214. **Penalty shot**

A special kind of penalty given when a player on defense breaks the rules in a big way to stop the other team from possibly scoring.

Examples include tripping an opponent who has a clear shot to score, throwing a stick, or a defender (except the goalie) using their hands on the puck. The player from the offense gets a chance to start with the puck at the middle of the ice and go directly towards the goal to try to score against the goalie by themselves.

215. **Pest**

A player who annoys the other team by often hitting them, sometimes in ways that might not be allowed.

216. **Pigeon**

A player who is not very good. They just hang around the net and wait for someone else to do the hard work. They feed on the leftovers of their better teammates. They score goals by being in the right place at the right time.

217. **Pillows**

The big pads that a goalie wears on their legs.

218. **Pinch**

A move to keep the hockey puck within the attacking area.

219. **Pipes**

The goal posts, the metal bars that make up the frame of the goal net.

220. **Pizza**

A terrible pass that goes through the center of the ice, where it is easy for the other team to steal it. It's like giving them a free pizza because they don't have to work hard to get it.

221. **Playmaker**

1. A quick player who often helps set up more plays than they score goals. This player uses their speed and stability on the ice to create opportunities, usually depending on a sharp-shooter to score.

2. A player who manages to assist in three goals during a single game.

222. **Playoff beard**

When a hockey player decides not to shave during the playoff games, believing it will bring good luck, so they end up growing a beard.

223. **Plumber,** *or* **Pipe-Fitter,** *or* **Mucker**

A player who is not very skilled or flashy but works hard and does the dirty work for the team. A plumber will chase the puck, hit the opponents, and fight for possession in the tough areas of the ice.

224. **Plus-minus**

A measure used in hockey to track a player's or a team line's performance, showing if they were present on the ice for a goal scored against their team (minus) or for their own team (plus).

Goals made during a power-play or while a team is on a penalty kill aren't included in the plus-minus tally. However, if a team scores while playing with fewer players due to a penalty (shorthanded), it is counted.

225. **Point**

A spot on the ice where the defenders are usual-ly positioned. It's just inside the corners of the other team's blue line. Their goal is to prevent the hockey puck from going past the blue line into the middle area of the rink. Players who are really good at shooting from far away, like snipers, are usually placed at the points too.

226. **Poke check**

A move where you use your stick to jab the puck away from the other player.

227. **Pond hockey**

A type of hockey that happens outside, usually on a frozen pond or lake when it's winter. It's a lot like another game called shinny. Sometimes, if a team isn't playing as well as they should be, with all their energy and focus, someone might say they're "playing pond hockey" to show they're not being serious enough.

228. Post-game handshake

When players from opposite teams give each other handshakes after a game. They do this as a way to show respect. They stand in lines opposite each other in the middle of the ice and walk past each other, shaking hands with everyone from the other team.

In the NHL, post-game handshakes are special and mainly happen at the end of a playoff series, not during the regular season.

229. Power forward

A big, strong player who is good at scoring. This player is fast enough to chase the puck into the corners of the ice, strong enough to get the puck away from others, and skilled enough to pass it to a teammate in front of the goal.

230. **Power move**

When a player quickly uses their speed and strength to move towards the goal. They might skate along the side of the rink first, then suddenly turn sharply towards the goal to make their play.

231. **Power play**

When one team has more players on the ice than the other team because the other team has been given penalties, causing them to have fewer players.

232. **Press Y**

This comes from the EA Sports NHL video game series. When you press the Y button, it begins a fight in the game.

233. **Puck Hog**

A player who often keeps the puck to themselves instead of passing it to teammates.

234. **Puck Luck**

When the hockey puck bounces in a way that gives someone an advantage.

235. **Puck-bunny**

A girl who likes hockey players a lot. Some puck-bunnies are really into hockey and know all the rules and stats, but others only care about the players.

236. **Pull the goalie**

When a team takes their goalie off the ice to add another player who is good at scoring. It's a move teams use only when they really need to catch up because they're behind by one goal and there's not much time left in the game.

237. **Pull The Trigger**

Shooting the puck.

238. **Pylon**

A term used to describe a very slow player who is usually easy to avoid and get past.

239. **Quarterback**

An offensive defenceman who plays one of the points on the power play and is skilled at skating and handling the puck.

240. **Quick whistle**

When the game is paused briefly because the referee can't see the puck, even though it's still in motion or can be played. This often happens when it looks like the goalie has caught the puck, but it's actually still moving and can be reached by players from the other team. In such cases, the referee ends the play by blowing the whistle, even though some players can still see the puck.

241. **Ragdolled**

When a player gets hit so hard during a game that they fall limp, similar to a floppy ragdoll.

242. **Razor**

A player who is performing at their best.

243. **Rebound**

When, after someone tries to score, the puck hits and bounces off the goalie, a player, the net, or sometimes even the boards behind the goal line.

244. **Red line**

The line that runs across the center of the ice rink, splitting it into two equal parts.

245. **Referee's crease**

A half-circle shaped area by the red line near the scorer's bench. During a game pause, if a referee is in this space, players are not allowed to step in.

246. **Ride the pine**

To sit on the bench for most or all of the game.

247. **Right wing**

A player who lines up on the right side of the center during a game when teams have an equal number of players on the ice. This position is similar to the left wing, who plays on the opposite side.

248. **Ringer**

When a significant better player is brought into a casual or tournament hockey game in a way that's not fair or allowed. When a Ringer plays very well, it can cause a lot of chaos in the game.

249. **Ringing The Iron**

When the puck strikes the goalpost.

250. **Rink**

The area where the game is played.

251. **Rink Rat**

A person who really enjoys spending time at the ice skating rink.

252. **Rink Swamp**

When the Zamboni machine puts too much water on the ice, making it too wet.

253. **Road Apple**

An old term that means frozen horse manure, which was once used as a puck.

254. **Rocket**

A very attractive woman (or man) who is watching the game from the stands.

255. **Rolling puck**

When the puck flips on its side and rolls.

256. **Roughing**

When a player hits an opponent with their hand or fist as if punching them during the game. This move is not allowed and results in a penalty.

257. **Salad**

A term for good-looking hair that is not as long as flow or lettuce.

258. **Saucer pass,** *or* **Sauce**

A type of pass in a game where one player sends the puck flying through the air to another player. It gets its name because the puck looks like a flying saucer while it's moving through the air. This pass is skillfully made just above the ice surface, high enough to go over an opponent's stick blade.

259. **Saucy paws,** *or* **silky mitts,**
or **soft hands**

A player who can handle the puck smoothly and make quick, precise passes or shots. They're a joy to watch and a nightmare to defend against.

260. **Save**

To block the puck from going into the net, stopping the other team from getting a point.

261. **Scoring chance**

When a team or player has an opportunity to score a goal.

262. **Screen**

Λ move in which a player from the attacking team stands in front of the goalie, blocking their view. It's a legal and strategic move, provided the player doesn't touch or interfere with the goalie.

263. **Screened shot**

A shot not visible to the goalie because other players are blocking their view.

264. **Send it,** *or* **Send him**

Shouted to let someone know there's a teammate who is in a good position to score or create a scoring chance.

265. **Shaft**

The long, straight portion of the stick that the player holds onto.

266. **Sharpshooter**

Someone who scores a lot of goals and is an accurate shooter.

267. **Shift**

The amount of time a player, team line, or group working on defense spends playing on the ice before another group comes in to take their place.

268. **Shinny**

A kind of hockey, often played on a pond, where players aim to keep the puck low, under knee height, because most are not wearing protective gear on their legs.

269. **Shootout**

When a game ends in a tie, even after extra time, teams take turns trying to score goals without any defenders except the goalie. This happens in regular season NHL games to decide the winner.

270. **Shorthanded**

When one team has less players playing on the ice compared to the other team because one or more of their players were given a penalty.

271. **Shortside**

The part of the goal that is nearest to the person trying to score.

272. **Shot on goal**

This term refers to any attempt to score that would successfully go into the net if the goalie doesn't block it. Attempts that miss completely or only hit the net's side aren't considered shots on goal. Also, if a shot strikes a goalpost or crossbar and doesn't actually go through into the goal, it doesn't count. Likewise, if the goalie stops a shot that, in the official scorer's opinion, wouldn't have scored anyway, it's not counted as a shot on goal.

273. **Shutdown pair**

Two players, either forwards or defensemen, that team up mainly to block or prevent the other team's offensive players from scoring.

274. **Shutdown player**

A player who is really good at stopping others from scoring.

275. **Sieve**

A goalie with many gaps in their defense, allowing the other team to score easily.

276. **Sin bin**

A term used to refer to the penalty box.

277. **Skatemill**

A machine used to practice skating skills.

278. **Skater**

A player on the ice who is not the goalie.

279. **Slapshot**

A powerful shot, often made with a large swing, where the player presses their stick down on the ice and uses the energy from the bent stick to shoot the puck quickly.

280. **Slashing**

When a player swings and hits another player's body or their stick. This is against the rules and results in a penalty.

281. **Slew foot**

When a player uses their foot to push or kick another player's skate out from under them, or trips them from behind, making them fall backwards. This move can lead to a match penalty.

282. Slot

The space right in front of the goalie, between the face-off circles. It's a prime spot for scoring goals because you have a clear shot at the net and can catch the goalie off guard.

283. Slow whistle

When a referee takes longer than usual to blow their whistle for a stoppage in a game, compared to similar situations.

284. Snap shot

The snap shot aims to blend the best parts of both the wrist shot (which is good for being accurate and fast) and the slap shot (which is known for the speed of the puck). In a snap shot, you don't pull back for a big swing like in a slap shot, and there's hardly any motion after the shot.

285. **Snarl**

An aggressive "growl" that players will do before a fight.

286. **Snipe**

A shot that goes right into the net without the goalie even touching it.

287. **Sniper**

This is a player who is really good at making precise and strong shots, often scoring points. The word comes from the military, where it describes someone who is very good at hitting targets from far away.

288. Snow Shower

When a player, upset about a goalie stopping their shot, purposely slides quickly to a stop in front of the goal. This action causes ice to spray up and cover the goalie. It's done on purpose to show frustration and can result in a penalty.

289. Spearing

The aggressive action of poking or thrusting at an opponent using the blade end of the stick. It results in at least a double-minor penalty.

290. Special teams

The group of players who participate during the power play periods and when the team is playing with fewer players due to penalties.

291. Spin-o-rama

A term created by sports announcer Danny Gallivan. It describes a hockey player making tight circles while keeping the puck under control with their stick, making it hard for other players to catch or stop them. Right now, using this move during NHL shootouts is not allowed.

292. Stack the pads

A move where the goalie falls to one side and blocks the puck by stacking their leg pads on top of each other.

293. Standing on his/her head

Used when a goalie is playing very well and making incredible saves.

294. Standup goalie

A type of goalie who prefers staying upright on their skates when facing a shot, unlike a butterfly goalie who might drop to the ground.

295. Stay-at-home defenseman

A defenseman who focuses primarily on defensive play rather than attacking. They rarely move the puck into the offensive zone themselves, preferring to pass to teammates. Typically, they are the last to exit their defensive area.

296. Stick checking

When a player uses their stick to block or mess with another player's stick.

297. Stickhandling

When someone uses their hockey stick to keep control of the puck as they move around other players.

298. Stickwork

The use of the stick in a way that is aggressive and not allowed because it can cause severe harm. This includes actions like cross-checking, high-sticking, hooking, slashing, spearing, and specific forms of tripping that involve the stick.

299. Stoned

A fantastic shot, but an even more amazing save.

300. **Stripes,** *or* **Zebra**

The referees or linesmen who officiate the game. It comes from the fact that they wear black and white striped uniforms.

301. **Strong Side**

The part of the ice where most of the players are, also usually where the puck is.

302. **Sucker**

A person known for getting scared easily, especially someone who tends to stay away from conflicts or fights.

303. **Sucker-punched**

A term used in hockey to describe when someone gets punched without being able to defend themselves. They might have been down on the ice or looking away. A cheap hit.

304. **Suicide pass,** *or* **Suey**

A pass that puts the receiver in a dangerous position, usually exposing them to a hard hit from an opponent.

305. **Sunburned**

A term used to mock a goalie who allows many goals to be scored against them. The joke is that the red light behind the net, which turns on every time a goal is scored, is like the sun, giving them a sunburn.

306. **Sweater**

Another name for a hockey jersey, the shirt players wear over their protective gear.

307. **Synthy**

A synthetic ice surface.

308. **Tag up**

When players go back to the neutral area after a linesman indicates there's been a delayed offside.

309. **Take a look**

Said to the player who has the puck to tell them they're not under pressure and have time to make a decision. They can either look for a teammate open for a pass or skate with the puck to create a scoring opportunity.

310. **Tap-in**

A shot taken very close to the goal that none of the opposing team's players or the goalie can stop or catch.

311. **Tape-to-tape**

A pass that is so accurate and smooth that it lands directly on the receiver's stick without bouncing or sliding off.

312. **Tendy,** *or* **Tender,** *or* **Netminder**

The goaltender, the player who guards the net and tries to stop the opposing team from scoring.

313. **Test the goalie**

To shoot on goal, trying to score.

314. **The show**

A term that hockey players use to refer to the highest level of professional hockey, such as the NHL or the AHL.

315. **Threading the needle**

A skillful move by an offensive player. It involves skating past multiple defenders and then taking a shot on goal. The term comes from the analogy of passing a thread through the eye of a needle, which requires precision and finesse.

316. **Tic-tac-toe**

A series of quick and accurate passes (tape-to-tape passes).

317. **Tilly**

A massive fight that breaks out during a hockey game.

318. **Time**

A term usually shouted to indicate that a teammate has enough time and space to control the puck and make a decision without pressure

319. Toe drag

Moving the puck on the ice by using the tip (toe) of the hockey stick's blade, instead of pushing it with the stick's bottom side.

320. Toepick

When someone falls because the front part of their ice skate sticks into the ice too sharply.

321. Top cheese, *or* Top cheddar

The two top corners of the goal.

322. Top shelf, *or* Where does mama keep the cookies

The upper part of the net, just below the cross-bar.

323. **Traffic**

A situation where many players from both teams are crowded in front of the net.

324. **Trap,**
or **Neutral zone trap**

A way of playing defense in hockey where a team places several players in the middle area of the rink. This makes it tough for the other team to move past the halfway line and enter their offensive area.

325. **Trapezoid**

A special area shaped like a trapezoid found just behind the goal line and the goal in NHL hockey. It's the only place behind the goal where the goalie is allowed to handle the puck. If the goalie touches the puck outside this area, behind the goal line, they get a minor penalty for delaying the game.

326. **Tripping**

When someone makes another person fall by hitting their legs or feet with a stick or any body part. It's not allowed and leads to a penalty.

327. **Turnbuckle**

The part at both ends of a hockey rink where the edge of the protective glass is cushioned and connects to the wall at a sharp corner. There have been incidents where players got hit into the turnbuckles and got badly hurt. To make the game safer, the NHL changed these sharp corners to curves.

328. **Turnover**

When the puck is accidentally given to the opposing team.

329. **Turnstile**

When a defenseman is easily bypassed by an opposing player, much like how one passes through a turnstile.

330. **Turtle**

A situation where one of the players involved in a fight does not want to participate and tries to protect himself by crouching or falling to his knees and covering his head and body with his arms.

331. **Twig**

Another name for a hockey stick. The term comes from the fact that hockey sticks used to be made of wood.

332. **Twine Bulge**

When the puck strikes the net with so much force that the net bulges outwards.

333. **Two-man advantage,** *or* **5-on-3**

When one team has two of its players put in the penalty box for breaking rules. Because of this, their team only has three players on the ice compared to the other team's five players. This does not count the goalkeepers.

334. **Two-way forward**

A forward who is good at both attacking during the game and defending their own goal.

335. **Umbrella**

A strategy a team on offense uses, especially when they have a powerplay advantage. It involves having five players spread out in a specific way in the area they're trying to score. They set up in a shape that looks like an umbrella around the other team's goal. One player stays back a bit, two are positioned along the sides, and two more are right in front of the goal.

336. **Unsportsmanlike**

A behavior by a player that the referee decides is a minor offense, leading to a 2-minute penalty, but not serious enough to require a larger penalty of 10 minutes or a game expulsion.

337. **Video goal judge**

A person who is not on the ice but checks if a goal is valid by watching a video replay.

338. **War room**

A special office located at the league's main offices in Toronto, where officials watch and analyze game footage.

339. **Wave Off**

When a referee cancels, "waves off," a goal that is not valid, or "waves off" a penalty.

340. **Wheel**

To skate fast with the puck. It is usually shouted by a team mate who sees an opportunity for the puck carrier to create a scoring chance by outskating the opponents.

341. **Wheelhouse**

The area right around a player's feet and straight across the player's shoulders, where it's best for the player to have the puck to hit it as hard as possible with a slap shot.

342. **Wholesale change**

When a team decides to replace all players on the ice, including both the forwards and defensemen, with new ones. A total of five players, made up of three forwards and two defensemen, are swapped out simultaneously.

343. **Windmill**

A spectacular save by a goalie who moves both their arms and legs to stop the puck, making it look like they are spinning like a windmill.

344. **Winger**

A playing position in hockey where the player mainly plays near the edges of the ice rink. A winger can either play on the right side, called a right winger, or on the left side, known as a left winger, depending on which side they are responsible for.

345. **Woody**

A type of stick made from wood, used in the past. Nowadays, sticks are crafted from very light and durable materials.

346. **Wrap-around,** *or* **Wrapper**

A type of goal in ice hockey that involves skating with the puck behind the opponent's net and then shooting it from the other side.

347. **Wrist shot,** *or* **Wrister**

A way of hitting the puck in hockey where you mostly use your wrist and forearm muscles to push it forward from the curved part at the bottom of the stick.

348. **Yard-sale,** *or* **Yardie**

A situation where a player is hit so hard by an opponent that he loses his equipment, such as his gloves, helmet, and stick, and they are scattered on the ice like items for sale at a yard sale.

349. Zamboni Confetti

The ice shavings that are gathered by the Zamboni machine.

350. Zone

A term that refers to any of the three sections into which the ice rink is divided by blue lines. These are identified as the attacking zone, neutral zone, or defensive zone.

the end!

501 HOCKEY FACTS
FOR SMART KIDS

Thank you so much for reading all the way to the end!

I really appreciate the time you took to give my book a read.

You could have picked from millions of other books but you took a chance and chose this one!

As a small indie publisher, it makes me really happy to be able to create and share books like this. So, I hope you enjoyed it!

If you have 60 seconds, it would mean the world to me to hear your honest feedback on Amazon. It does wonders for the book and I love hearing your experience with it.

To leave your feedback:

1. Open your camera app

2. Point your mobile device at the QR code below

3. The review page will appear in your web browser

Or

Click "Your Orders" in your Amazon account page

Thank you!